A Special Gift

To: _____

From: _____

Date: _____

Peace on Earth

A Celebration of Christmas

Edited & Compiled by

Caroline Brownlow

A Childlike Faith

Whatever else be lost among the years,
Let us keep Christmas still a shining thing:
Whatever doubts assail us, or what fears,
Let us hold close one day, remembering
It's poignant meaning in the hearts of men.
Let us get back our childlike faith again.

Grace Noll Crowell

*W*hat is a true gift?
One for which nothing
is expected in return.

Ancient Proverb

May joy come

from heaven above

to all those who

Christmas love!

❧✳❧

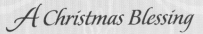

A Christmas Blessing

May God grant you the light in Christmas,
which is faith; the warmth of Christmas,
which is love; the radiance of Christmas,
which is purity; the righteousness of
Christmas, which is justice; the belief in
Christmas, which is truth; the all of
Christmas, which is Christ.

Wilda English

The Christmas Story

And there were shepherds living out in the fields nearby, keeping watch over their flock at night. An angel of the Lord appeared to them, and the glory of the Lord shone around them, and they were terrified. But the angel said to them, "Do not be afraid. I bring you good news of great joy that will be for all the people. Today in the town of David a Savior has been

born to you; he is Christ the Lord. This will be a sign to you: You will find a baby wrapped in strips of cloth and lying in a manger."

Suddenly a great company of the heavenly host appeared with the angel, praising God and saying, "Glory to God in the highest, and on earth peace to men on whom his favor rests."

Luke 2:8-14

Christmas
is not a date.
It is a state
of mind.

Mary Ellen Chase

I Hope You Carol

The word "carol" is derived
from the old French word
"caroler," which means dancing
around in a circle. It was
derived from the Latin "caraula,"
which in turn was derived from the
Greek "choraules."

I Love Christmas!

I love Christmas time, and yet
I notice this each year I live;
I always like the gifts I get,
But how I love the gifts I give!

Carolyn Wells

*Selfishness makes
Christmas a burden;
love makes it a delight.*
Anonymous

Love one another deeply
from the heart.
1Peter 1:22

Christmas Every Day

My Dad taught me something about Christmas I shall never forget. In the midst of the chaos we called Christmas, Daddy would load us all in the car and we'd go to the poorest neighborhood in town with food and presents.

He had notified the family beforehand they were about to be invaded, but they were always still surprised! It was always more than they expected. The best part of all – this was no once a year, feel good gesture. My Dad did this all the time. He brought people home for dinner or to spend the night. He took groceries and his repertoire of Bible jokes to people in need. He lived as if every day was Christmas. Would that we all could.

We all can give. Even the poorest human being has something to give that the richest cannot buy.

George M. Adams

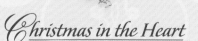

Christmas in the Heart

It's Christmas in the cottage,
Christmas in the mart;
But the dearest, truest Christmas
is the Christmas in the heart.

❧❋❧

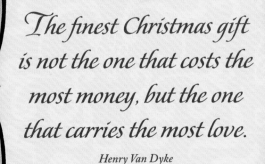

The finest Christmas gift
is not the one that costs the
most money, but the one
that carries the most love.

Henry Van Dyke

Christmas Joy

Joy to the world,
the Lord is come.
Let earth receive
her King!

Isaac Watts

Twinkle, Twinkle Little Star

For many years, Christmas trees were decorated with candles and candy, small dolls and paper ornaments, but all that would change by 1900.

In the 1870s, flat lead ornaments from Germany in the shape of stars, crosses, butterflies, etc. began appearing in stores for sale. Glass-blown ornaments also from Germany were imported, and by 1890 the 14 Woolworth stores were selling over 200,000 annually. The Sears Roebuck catalog carried them as well and successfully sold the beautiful glass-blown decorations by mail.

Because of the wartime embargo of German goods in 1918, North Americans had to begin producing their own glass ornaments. The result was a supply of simple round balls that were vastly inferior to the German product. However, by 1939 the Corning Company had perfected a mass-produced quality ornament that adorned the trees most of us grew up with.

During all this period, the candles on the tree had been replaced with electric lights. General Electric bought Thomas Edison's patent and light bulb factory, and in the 1890's began manufacturing special lights just for the tree. Other companies

jumped into the growing market and over the next 50 years the Christmas tree light evolved. Miniature lights were offered. Clear lights became colored lights by dipping them in lacquer. Faces of popular cartoon characters appeared. Lights "flashed," "bubbled," and then "twinkled." And finally the crowning achievement came when somebody made a string of lights that didn't go dead when just one bulb was out and would last more than two weeks. Now that was a real Christmas present!

It is Christmas in the heart that puts Christmas in the air.

Anonymous

To Be a Child

It is good to be children
sometimes, and never better
than at Christmas, when
its mighty Founder was
a child himself.

Charles Dickens

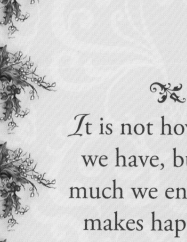

It is not how much
we have, but how
much we enjoy, that
makes happiness.

Charles H. Spurgeon

The Gift of Christmas Memories

This year, give yourself or your family the gift of Christmas memories:

Start a Christmas journal. Either purchase a beautiful one or create a handmade one, and fill it with stories, photos and memories.

Collect family recipes for all the special Christmas treats. Make copies, then wrap and distribute to all the family.

Have old family photos retouched and make copies, or have old 8mm home movies put on DVD for everyone.

Make a special journal for your children and grandchildren about what Christmas was like when you were young.

Spend time with family or friends telling Christmas stories and recalling your favorite Christmases.

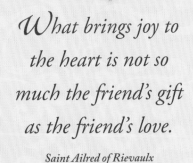

*What brings joy to
the heart is not so
much the friend's gift
as the friend's love.*

Saint Ailred of Rievaulx

A Joy Returned

Somehow not only for
Christmas but all the
Long years through, the
Joy that you give to
Others is the joy that
Comes back to you.

John Greenleaf Whittier

The Heart of Giving

The heart of the giver makes
the gift dear and precious.

Martin Luther

*He who has not Christmas
in his heart will never find it
under a tree.*

Roy L. Smith

Women Do Christmas

In case no one has noticed, women do Christmas. If there were no women in the world, there would be no Christmas. Women buy the presents, wrap them, cook all the food and decorate the house. Women do Christmas.

But I love Christmas – I really do! It comes at just the right time as the year is drawing to a close, and stores have all those fantastic sales.

It is a time when the world stops to celebrate the birth of a Baby whose actual birthday we'll never know. It is also a time of giving and forgiving, and expressing gratitude and renewing that sense of connectedness we all share.

Now you can't have all this and not be tired. But it's a good tired.

Starry, Starry Night

The stars were brighter than ever before.
The night was different, crackling with
new beginnings. Something was
happening in the dark, tiny stable;
the Gift of God was before us.

PCB

The simple shepherds heard the voice of an angel and found their Lamb; the wise men saw the light of a star and found their Wisdom.

Fulton J. Sheen

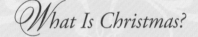

What Is Christmas?

What is Christmas?
It is tenderness for the past, courage for
the present, hope for the future. It is a
fervent wish that every cup may overflow
with blessings rich and eternal, and
that every path may lead to peace.

Agnes M. Pharo

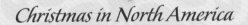

Christmas in North America

The very first Christmas celebration in North America, according to the records we have, predated the arrival of the Pilgrims. It occurred in 1607 in Jamestown, Virginia, where survivors of the 100 original settlers tried to raise their somber, uncertain spirits by saluting the birth of Christ in their small chapel. While they lacked all the elements of our modern-day celebrations, perhaps they captured the essence of the day more than most.

Our First Christmas

The first Christmas after we were married was memorable – for several reasons. We were young, still in college, poor and totally in love. We experienced the normal clash of Christmas cultures. I was from a large family, he was an only child. You get the picture.

But what I remember most was the Christmas tree in our tiny duplex. It was a scrawny, little thing no one else wanted. We didn't have any real Christmas decorations, so I cut out paper and felt snowmen, birds and angels to hang on the sparse branches. Never has a Christmas tree looked so pitiful, yet so full of love.

After 42 years, we still have a few of those ornaments. Some things have changed since that first Christmas together, but the most important things remain.

The Light

The light that shines
from the humble manger
is strong enough to lighten
our way to the end
of our days.

Author Unknown

After all, Christmas-living is the best
kind of Christmas-giving.

Henry Van Dyke

Behold I bring you good news
of great joy for all the people.

Luke 2:10

The First Christmas Cards

The first Christmas card was produced in England in 1843. John Calcott Horsley, a young but popular artist, designed the single panel card showing a large family celebrating Christmas dinner and two small scenes depicting the Victorians' concern for the less fortunate. Not more than 1000 cards were printed in black and white, and each was hand water-colored by William Mason.

Later the idea spread to America where in

1874 Louis Prang of Roxbury, Massachusetts, developed a color lithographic process using up to 20 different colors. Prang offered cash prizes ($2000 for first place) to artists each year to design his growing line of Christmas cards. The Americans loved his peaceful Madonnas, cherubs and charming children in nightshirts, while the English preferred his intricate floral patterns.

By 1900 the Christmas card market was flourishing. While the cards were only postcards with no envelopes, the colors were rich and often contained an embossing or even small ribbon.

The artwork was typically an idealized snowy landscape, or graceful children drawn by famous illustrators such as Frances Brundage or Ellen Clapsaddle.

Realizing the potential, a young boy from Nebraska with a shoebox full of his favorite postcards decided to enter the market in 1910. His name was Joyce Hall, and his company (Hallmark Cards) would pioneer the modern Christmas card mailed in an envelope. Later, they would dominate the market worldwide in more than 20 languages.

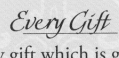

Every Gift

Every gift which is given,
even though it be
small,is great if given
with affection.

Pindar

The Spirit of Christmas

I am thinking of you today because it is Christmas, and I wish you happiness. And tomorrow, because it will be the day after Christmas, I shall wish you happiness, and so on through the year. I may not be able to tell you about it every day, because I may be far away, or both of us may be very busy, or perhaps I cannot afford to pay the postage on so many letters, or find the time to write them. But that makes no difference. The thought and the wish will be here just the same. In my work and in daily life, I will try not to be unfair to you or injure you in any way. In my pleasure, if we can be together, I would like to share the fun with you. Whatever joy or success comes to you will make me glad. Without pretense, and in plain words, good will to you is what I mean in the Spirit of Christmas.

Henry Van Dyke

When we throw out the Christmas tree, we should be especially careful not to throw out the Christmas spirit with it.

Anonymous